GANG WAY! The Mystery of Magnetism!

by Ailynn Collins

CAPSTONE PRESS
a capstone imprint

Published by Capstone Press, an imprint of Capstone
1710 Roe Crest Drive, North Mankato, Minnesota 56003
capstonepub.com

Library of Congress Cataloging-in-Publication Data is available on the Library of Congress website.

ISBN: 9798875214172 (hardcover)
ISBN: 9798875214196 (paperback)
ISBN: 9798875214202 (ebook PDF)

Summary: Magic is in the air as Scooby and the Mystery Inc. gang unravel the mystery of magnetism. From attracting and repelling forces and powerful poles to magnetic fields and electromagnets, uncover the magical secrets behind an invisible force.

Editorial Credits
Editor: Christopher Harbo; Designer: Tracy Davies; Media Researcher: Svetlana Zhurkin; Production Specialist: Whitney Schaefer

Image Credits
Bridgeman Images: Stefano Bianchetti, 7 (top); Getty Images: ZU_09, 26 (top); NASA: 29; Shutterstock: Africa Studio, 13 (nail), 23 (bottom), 24 and 27 (nail), Andi Berger, 27 (paper clips), Andrey_Popov, 6, Anton Petrychenko, 9, Artem Stepanov, 10 (plastic bottle), Berents, 27 (copper wire), BlueRingMedia (nail and wire), 27 (top), Cartooncux (beaker), cover and throughout, Craig Walton, 15 (bottom), cyo bo, 17 (bottom), DKN0049, 19, Dmitry Rukhlenko (paper clip), 13, 24, fokke baarssen, 28, Fotofermer, 10 (can), FoxGrafy, 21, gpwlsl302 (bar magnet), 17, 24, Graphic design (bottle cap), 10, 11, GraphicsRF (magnet), cover and throughout, greenphotoKK, 4 (iron filings), HobbitArt (science icons), cover and throughout, Honourr, 15 (top), K.K.T Madhusanka, 25 (back), Kolonko, 20, Kung37 (battery), 27 (bottom), Luciano Cosmo, 4 (gloved hand), MaraZe, 11 (meatball), Maria Martyshova (background), cover and throughout, Michael LaMonica, 23 (middle), New Africa, 8, 10 and 11 (fork), 17 (tape), Oksana Kurnosova, 17 (toy cars), Patricia F. Carvalho, 26 (middle), Pavel Aleks, 10 (jar), Probowening, 18, 22, redknapper (bar magnet), 13, 14, Robert Przybysz, 5, Rvector (battery), 27 (top), Santi Kuttawat (paper clip), 10, 11, SeDmi, 10 (wooden stick), Sergei Kozachko, 25 (disco ball), Triff, 7 (bottom), Valery Evlakhov, 16 (magnets), Vectomart, 12, Vector FX (round magnet), 10, 11, Vector things, 4 (jar)

Printed and bound in China. PO 006276

Table of Contents

Magnetism Magic

While hanging out at home, the Mystery Inc. gang watches Shaggy perform a magic trick. In one hand, he holds a clear jar containing black sand. His other hand is wearing a glove. As Shaggy holds his gloved hand above the lid of the jar, the sand suddenly comes to life. It rises to the top of the jar. Then it falls back to the bottom when Shaggy moves his hand away.

Abracadabra!

Ooh! Magic!

Fred and Daphne clap. But Velma rubs her chin. She knows what's really happening. Shaggy is using the science of magnetism for his trick. The black "sand" is actually iron filings, and he has a magnet hidden inside his glove.

Shaggy's magic trick uses magnetism. But what is magnetism, exactly?

Magnetism is an invisible force that pushes and pulls objects. It works underwater and through solids. A strong magnet can even pull on an object through a table top!

Magnets can be found naturally as rocks or made from certain metals. Some things stick to or are attracted to magnets. Others aren't.

So, come on, gang! It's time to solve the mystery of magnetism—and that starts with a groovy history lesson!

Magnets were first discovered in ancient times. A Greek shepherd named Magnes was looking after his sheep when his metal staff stuck to a rock. Little did Magnes know, he had discovered magnetism! The element in that rock was later named magnetite.

FACT

Rocks made of magnetite are called lodestones. Lodestones were used in early compasses to help explorers find their way around the world.

Magnificent Magnets

Believe it or not, gang, magnets are everywhere! Look around your home. You're sure to find a bunch.

Check out your refrigerator. Do you have magnets holding up your artwork or family photos? Now open your refrigerator doors. There are magnets at work there too! Magnetic strips hold the doors shut to help keep the cold air sealed inside.

Did you just say you have a magnetic personality, Fred?

That's my story, and I'm *sticking* to it.

But don't stop at the refrigerator. Look for magnets in your toys and other common items. Board game pieces sometimes have magnets, and so do some belt clasps.

Magnets can also be found in some duvet covers, holding them neatly closed. And tiny magnets help store data inside your computer!

FACT

Microwaves use magnets to make electromagnetic waves to heat your food.

As you may already know, magnets stick to some items and not to others. Why is that? As it turns out, magnets only stick to things made of magnetic metals. Iron, nickel, and cobalt are three types of magnetic metals. Objects that contain some of these metals will stick to magnets.

Try a simple experiment to test what magnets will stick to. Gather a refrigerator magnet, a metal paper clip, a wooden craft stick, a soda can, a glass jar, a plastic bottle, a fork, and a metal bottle cap. Then, one by one, pass the magnet over each object.

What did you discover from this experiment?

You probably saw that the soda can, the jar, the wooden craft stick, and the plastic bottle didn't stick to the magnet. That's because of what these items are made of. Plastic, wood, glass, and aluminum are not made of magnetic materials.

Did the paper clip, bottle cap, and fork stick to the magnet? If so, they are magnetic because they contain steel. And steel is made with iron, which is a magnetic material. That's why they stuck to your magnet.

Magnets are magnificent, but what makes them work? The answer lies in atoms, the tiny units that make up all matter. Inside atoms are even tinier neutrons, electrons, and protons.

Electrons carry electrical charges. They spin like little tops. In most materials, half the electrons spin one way and half the other. This cancels out the magnetism of the material. But in some metals, all the electrons spin in one direction, making them magnetic.

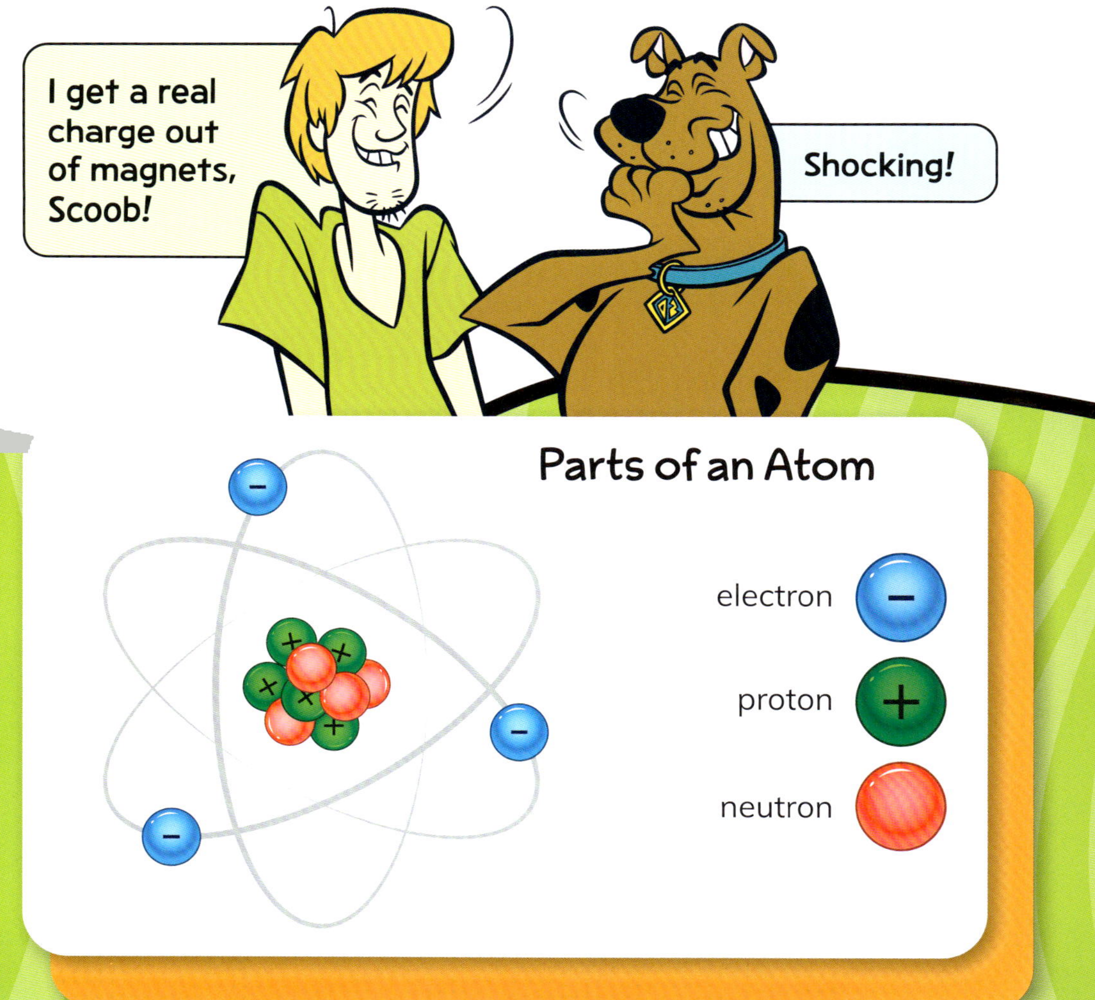

Iron, nickel, and cobalt all have electrons that spin in one direction. Not only are these metals magnet-loving materials, but they also can be used to make magnets!

Make a Magnet

WHAT YOU'LL NEED:

bar magnet
iron nail
paper clip

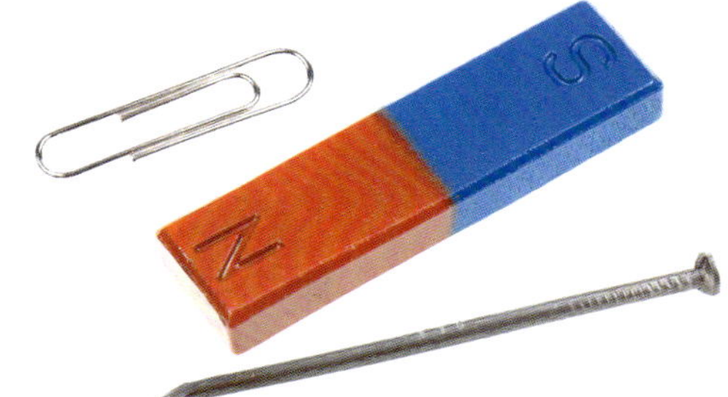

WHAT TO DO:

1. Stroke the bar magnet against the nail in one direction. Repeat this action about 30 times, and don't change directions.
2. Set the bar magnet aside.
3. Touch the nail to the paper clip and slowly lift. Watch what happens.

Did the nail pick up the paper clip? If so, the nail is acting like a magnet! Stroking the nail with the bar magnet made the mini-magnets inside the nail all line up together.

FACT

Magnets come in many shapes and sizes. The bar magnet is the most common. But there are also horseshoe magnets, disc magnets, and spherical magnets.

Powerful Poles

If you've ever played with magnets, you may have noticed something mysterious. When the ends of two magnets get close to each other, they either pull together or push apart. Pretty groovy, right? But why does this happen?

The mystery behind this pull and push lies in a magnet's poles. All magnets have a north pole and a south pole. And a magnet's power is strongest at these poles. So, when two poles meet, something big is bound to happen.

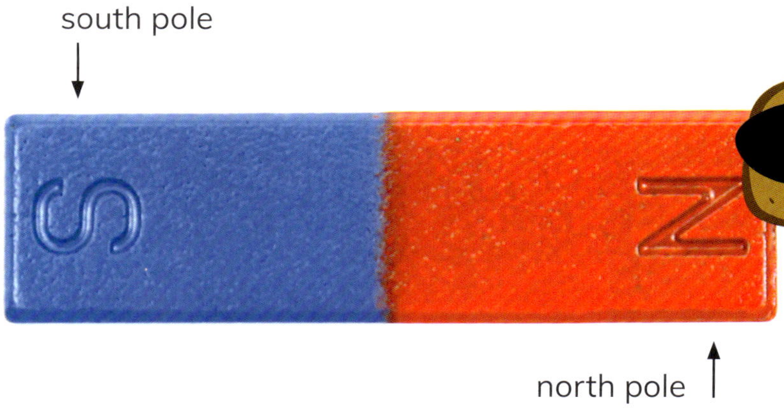

south pole

north pole

Try it yourself with two bar magnets. Slowly slide the blue end of one magnet toward the red end of the other. Watch the magnets pull closer to each other until—CLICK!—they stick together. Their opposite poles—one north and one south—are drawn to each other. Or, as we like to say, opposites attract.

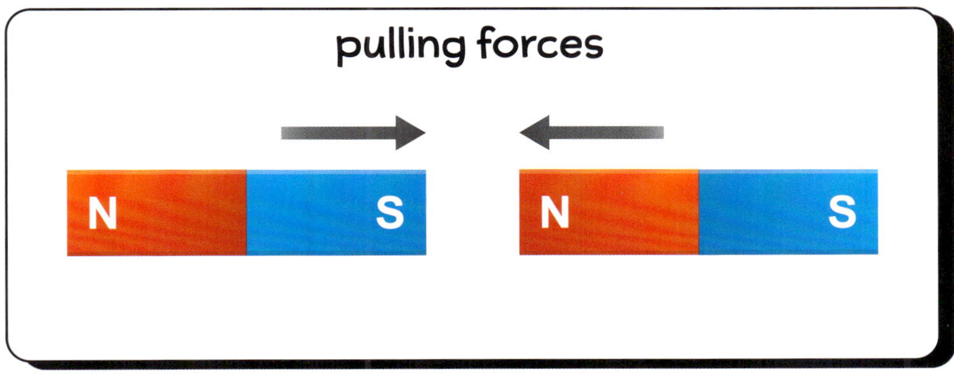

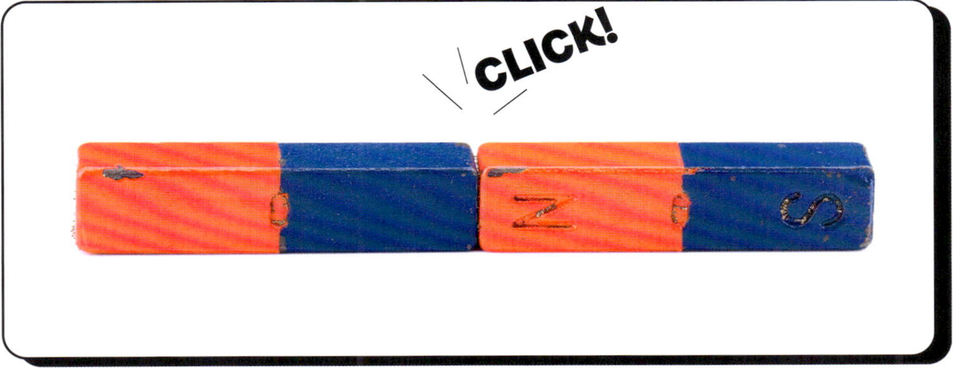

FACT

Some bar magnets have their north and south poles painted red and blue. Many also have the letters "N" and "S" marked on each end for north and south.

But what happens when you flip one of the bar magnets around? Let's find out. Slowly slide one magnet's blue end toward the second magnet's blue end. Watch as the second magnet scoots away from the first one. Their like poles—both south poles—push away from each other. In other words, like poles repel.

Magnetic Push Power Race

WHAT YOU'LL NEED:

tape
4 bar magnets
2 toy cars
a friend

WHAT TO DO:

1. Tape one bar magnet to the top of a toy car. Allow either the north or south pole of the magnet to hang off the back of the car slightly.
2. Repeat step 1 with the other toy car.
3. Set the cars on a hard floor at one end of a room.
4. Give your friend one of the two remaining bar magnets. You can take the other one.
5. At the same time, hold the repelling ends of the bar magnets close to the back ends of your cars. Try to use their pushing power to move your cars across the room.
6. See who can get their car across the room first!

A train that runs on magnets that repel each other is called a maglev train. It gets its power from magnetic levitation!

The Mysterious Magnetic Field

Magnetism may be invisible, but there is a way to see its power. Put a bar magnet on a table and cover it with a piece of paper. Then sprinkle iron filings over the paper.

Do you see how the iron filings form circles around each end of the magnet? This is what scientists call the magnetic field. This area around the magnet is where the magnetic force is felt. It's an invisible force field that moves outward from the magnet.

Iron filings on top of paper covering a bar magnet

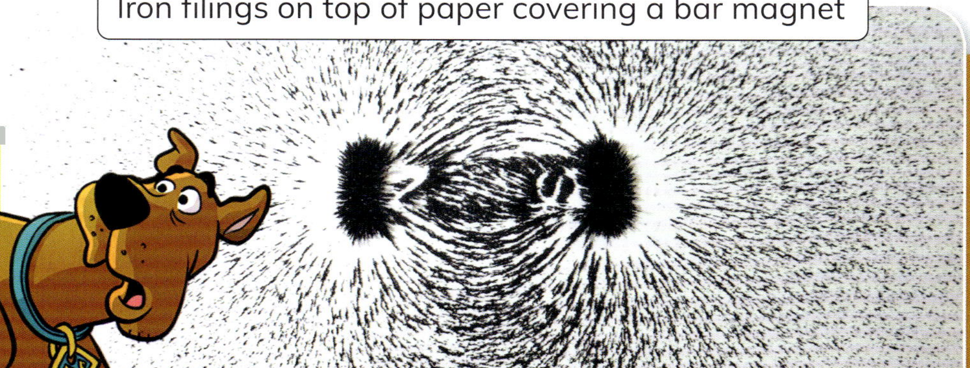

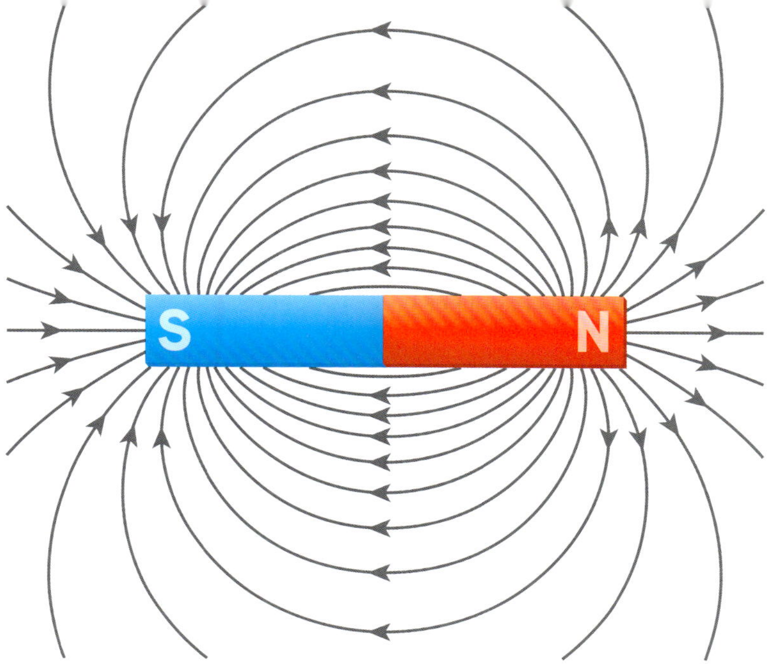

magnetic field lines

Most of the filings are gathered around the poles because that's where the field is the strongest. But some of the filings curve between the poles too. If you drew the paths of the filings, they would look like curved lines. Scientists call these field lines. Field lines show the direction of the magnetic force.

Field lines start at one pole and move toward the other pole—but they never cross each other. And any magnetic metal objects that pass within these field lines are attracted to the magnet. They experience the magnetic force.

FACT

Iron filings are tiny, powder-like pieces of iron. They're great for doing experiments and magic tricks!

Can you guess what makes up the biggest magnet in the world? The answer is *in* the question. It's our world!

The Earth is a giant—but weak—magnet! It has north and south magnetic poles. As a result, there's a giant magnetic field around the whole planet.

Earth's magnetic field

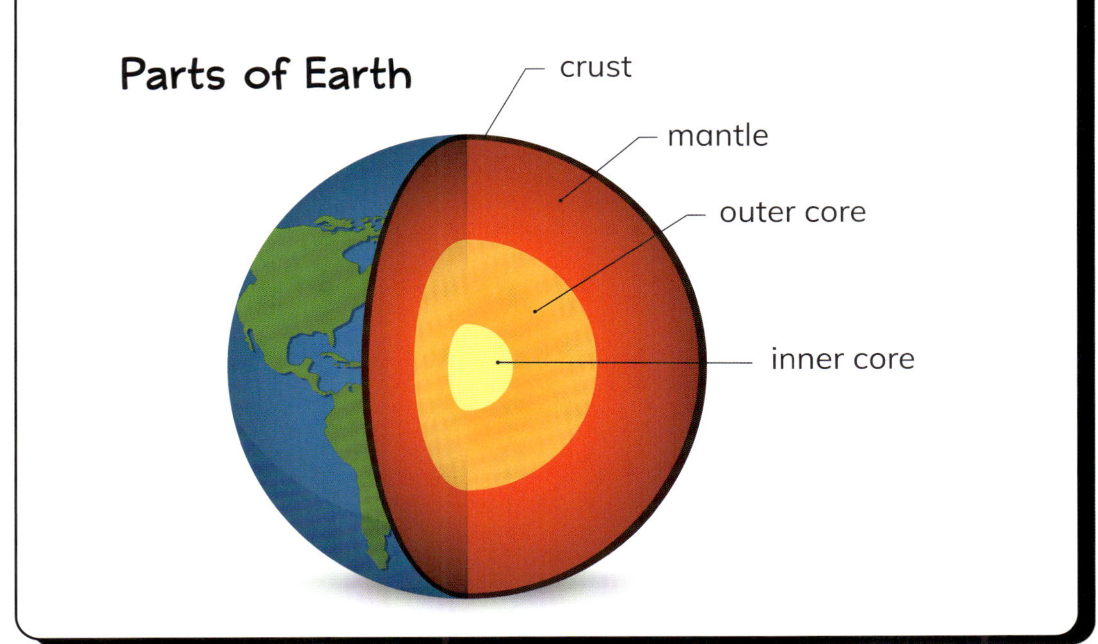

What makes Earth a giant magnet? At its center sits a solid inner core made of iron, nickel, and other elements. Around the inner core lies a swirling outer core of molten iron, nickel, and other elements. The outer core's swirling motion acts like a magnetism engine that turns the planet into a giant magnet.

If you've ever used a compass, you've seen how the north end of the needle points toward Earth's North Pole. But remember, opposite poles attract! That means the magnetic pole near Earth's North Pole is actually a south magnetic pole! And the one near the South Pole is really a north magnetic pole. Now that's pretty groovy!

FACT

Northern and southern lights happen when charged particles from the sun are redirected by Earth's magnetic field.

Permanent and Temporary Magnets

Alright, gang! Up until now, we've mainly talked about permanent magnets. These are magnets that stay magnetic for a long time. If you break or heat them to a high temperature, they can lose their magnetism. But otherwise, they last almost forever.

Iron filings on top of paper covering a broken magnet

All permanent magnets are made of ferromagnetic materials. These materials attract magnetic metals.

A lodestone is a natural magnet that is made of magnetite. It is one example of a permanent magnet. Your refrigerator magnets—which often contain a highly magnetic material called barium ferrite—are another example.

But would you believe that some magnets don't have their power all the time? It's true! These are known as temporary magnets.

Do you remember the activity when you turned a nail into a magnet? You were actually making a temporary magnet by stroking it with a bar magnet. The nail could pick up paper clips for a few minutes. But eventually, it likely lost its magnetism and went back to being an ordinary nail.

Electromagnets are also temporary magnets. They become magnets when they are given a special power—electricity!

To understand how this works, let's first talk about electricity. Remember how all matter is made of atoms? Inside those atoms are positively charged protons, neutral neutrons, and negatively charged electrons. Electricity is what happens when the tiny electrons start to dance around. When they move between atoms, an electric current is produced.

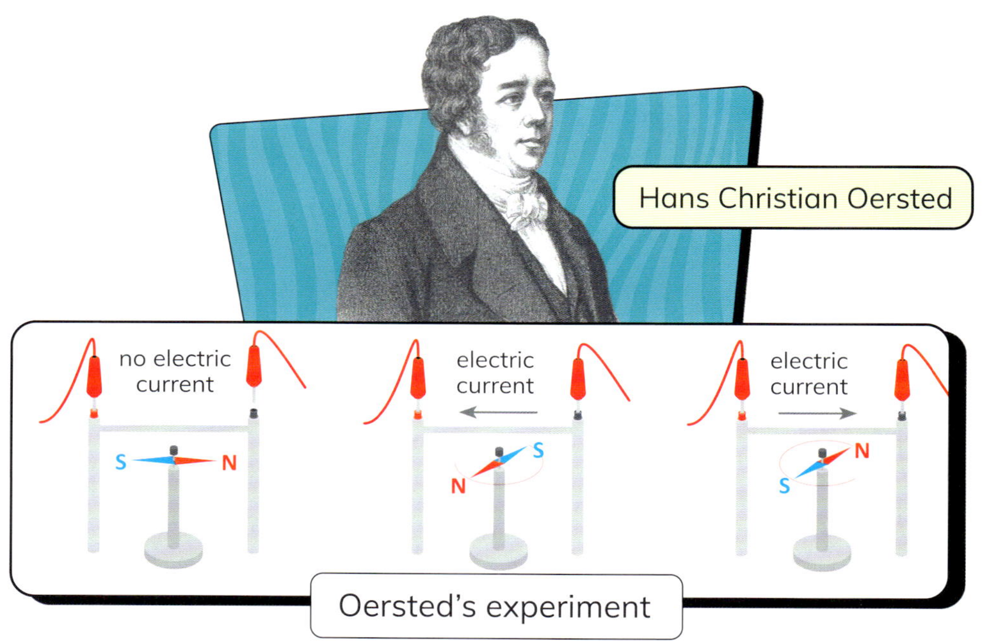

Oersted's experiment

In 1820, a scientist named Hans Christian Oersted moved a compass near an electric current. When he saw the compass needle move away from pointing north, he realized electric currents produce their own magnetic field. This field attracted the compass needle and moved it away from its usual position.

In time, scientists learned more about the relationship between electricity and magnetism. They discovered that a piece of iron coiled with wire became a magnet when an electric current passed through the wire. When the electric current stopped, the iron lost its magnetic power. They called this phenomenon electromagnetism.

FACT

In 1824, British scientist William Sturgeon built the first electromagnet. His small electromagnet was able to lift 9 pounds (4.1 kilograms) of iron.

Make an Electromagnet

WHAT YOU'LL NEED:

iron nail

copper wire

AA battery

metal paper clips

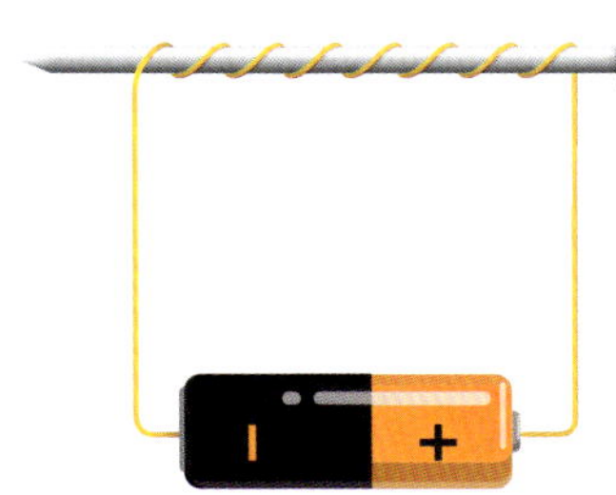

WHAT TO DO:

1. Wrap the entire length of the nail with the wire. Make sure the wire is tightly and closely wound. Leave an inch (2.5 centimeters) or more of wire free at each end.
2. Place one end of the wire on the + side of the battery and the other on the – side.
3. Watch what happens to paper clips placed next to the nail. As electricity flows through the wire, the nail will attract them.
4. Remove the wire from the battery. What happens to the paper clips now?

When the wire is attached to the battery, the electrical current passing through the wire turns the nail into a magnet. When you pull the wire away from the battery, electricity stops flowing. The paper clips fall away because the nail loses its electromagnetic power.

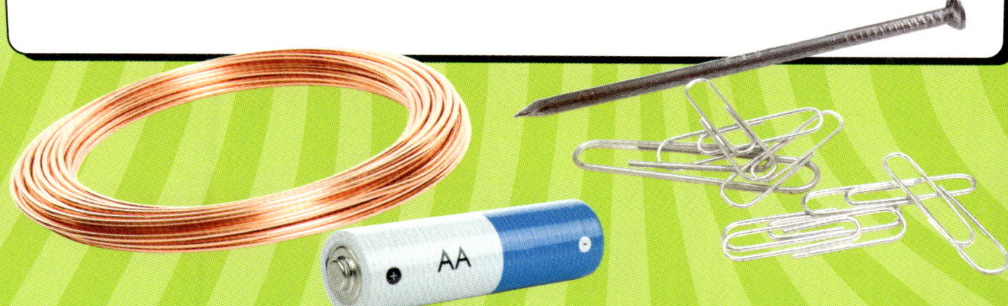

Useful Magnets

Magnets are super useful! In a junkyard, electromagnets pick up and sort through huge pieces of metal. These giant magnets are also used to pluck magnetic materials from landfills and recycling plants.

Magnets help save lives too. They're used in Magnetic Resonance Imaging (MRI) machines in hospitals. These machines use magnets to help doctors detect tumors, strokes in the brain, and injuries in the muscles and other tissues.

Magnets are also used to turn wind energy into electricity. When the wind blows, it turns the blades on a wind turbine. A turbine has a generator with magnets and a coil of wire inside. As the magnets move, they create an electric current in the wire. This current can supply electricity to nearby homes and businesses.

Magnets are useful off our planet too! In the International Space Station, they are used to keep experiments steady and prevent things from shaking about too much. Magnets are also used to keep spacecraft from getting lost. They orient the spaceships to Earth's magnetic field.

Scientists are even trying to see if giant magnets can be used to clean up space junk. Now that's far out!

GLOSSARY

atom (AT-uhm)—the smallest particle of an element

compass (KUHM-puhs)—an instrument used for finding directions

current (KUHR-uhnt)—a flow of electrons through an object

force (FORS)—any action that changes the movement of an object

iron filings (EYE-urn FYE-lings)—very small pieces of iron that look like a dark gray powder

orient (OR-ee-ent)—to set in any determined position, especially in relation to the points of a compass

permanent (PUR-muh-nuhnt)—lasting for a long time or forever

phenomenon (fe-NOM-uh-non)—something very unusual or remarkable

radiation (ray-dee-AY-shuhn)—waves of energy sent out by sources of heat or light, or by radioactive material

temporary (TEM-puh-rer-ee)—lasting only a short time

turbine (TUR-bine)—a machine with blades that can be turned by moving steam, water, or air

READ MORE

Bailey, Jacqui. *Let's Investigate Magnets.* New York: Crabtree Publishing Company, 2021.

Collins, Ailynn. *Understanding Magnetism in Max Axiom's Lab.* North Mankato, MN: Capstone Press, 2025.

Troup, Roxanne. *Magnets.* New York: DK Publishing, 2023.

INTERNET SITES

Britannica Kids: Magnets and Magnetism
kids.britannica.com/kids/article/Magnet-and-Magnetism/353411

Ducksters: Physics for Kids—Magnetism
ducksters.com/science/magnetism.php

Time for Kids: What Are Magnets?
timeforkids.com/g34/what-are-magnets-2

INDEX

ABOUT THE AUTHOR

Ailynn Collins has written many books for children, from stories about aliens and monsters, to books about science, space, and the future. These are her favorite subjects. She lives outside Seattle with her family and five dogs. When she's not writing, she enjoys participating in dog shows and dog sports.